affirmations for self-love and healing

by emily juniper

I think we've all struggled with self-love from time to time. I never heard the term self-love (now, a popular buzzword) until I was in my mid-twenties, and it's hard to practice something you can't even name.

One of the ways we can practice self-love is positive self-talk. Reciting an empowering phrase, affirming your worth, or jotting down the things you like about yourself are all ways you can practice positive self-talk. Tell yourself you're a beautiful, intelligent, strong being who is full of potential each and every day, and eventually, you'll start to believe it.

This book of affirmations will serve as gentle, positive reminders to anyone interested in recovery, self-care, and healing. Read one each day, share them with your friends, or rip the pages out and paste them in places where you'll see them.

Remember, learning how to love yourself is a journey, and even one small step each day will lead you in the right direction.

Be gentle with you.

xx, emily j.

Part 1: For the healing heart

Stop letting people treat you like a

secret

when you know damn well you're a

revelation.

THE BROKEN
BONES?
THE ACHING
HEART?
THEY HURT
BECAUSE THEY'RE
HEALING.

If the time wasn't right, the person wasn't either.

Believe that.

I deserve so much more

than a love

that comes only

in WAVES.

You are allowed

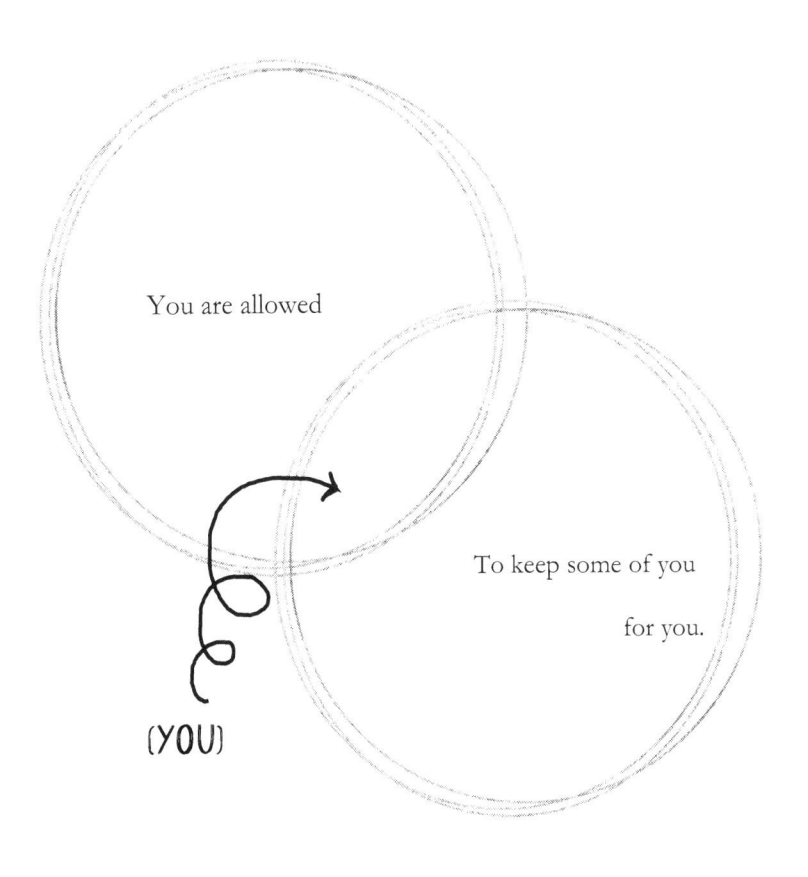

(YOU)

To keep some of you

for you.

I am hard to love

sometimes,

but that

doesn't make me

less worthy.

NEVER FEEL AS THOUGH THE
LOVE YOU GAVE THEM WAS A
WASTE OF TIME.

HAVEN'T YOU HEARD?

ENERGY CAN ONLY BE
CHANGED,

BUT NEVER LOST.

I AM WORTHY OF LOVE I AM WORTHY OF LOVE.

I am not a stock.

My value does not decrease when someone else doesn't find me worthy of their love.

Stop handing the one who cut you
the needle and thread to
stitch you up.

The one who hurt you
cannot heal you,
too.

Poison does not
become antidote
overnight.

IT IS OKAY TO MISS SOMEONE WHO HURT YOU.

(IT IS OKAY <u>NOT</u> TO FORGIVE SOMEONE WHO HURT YOU, TOO)

And that's the funny thing about heartbreak.

You're always stronger on the other side.

A CHECKLIST FOR THE HURTING HEART:

- [ ] CRY
- [ ] VENT
- [ ] CRY SOME MORE
- [ ] WALLOW, EAT COMFORT FOOD, AND BINGE NETFLIX, HULU, ETC.
- [ ] CRY AGAIN
- [ ] TAKE CUTE SELFIES
- [ ] SURROUND YOURSELF WITH PEOPLE WHO LOVE YOU
- [ ] MAKE 1 OR 2 SPONTANEOUS (BUT NOT RECKLESS) DECISIONS
- [ ] CREATE SOMETHING BEAUTIFUL
- [ ] TALK TO A PROFESSIONAL

- Cry a bit more ☐
- Travel somewhere new ☐
- Pray or connect with the spiritual world in some way ☐
- Volunteer ☐
- Get outside (nature has healing powers) ☐
- Cry juuuust a little more ☐
- Wait... ☐
- ... ☐
- ... ☐
- ... ☐
- (It get's better, doesn't it?) ☐

It's time you see yourself for the masterpiece you are.

They are not the ocean,

<u>YOU</u> are the ocean.

They were just a ship you allowed to crash upon your shores.

Remember,

you cannot make a mosaic

without a few broken

pieces.

Repeat after me:

I am enough and I am not too much. I am enough and I am not too much. I am enough and I am not too much. I am enough and I am not too much. I am enough and I am not too much. I am enough and I am not too much. I am enough and I am not too much. I am enough and I am not too much. I am enough and I am not too much. I am enough and I am not too much. I am enough and I am not too much. I am enough and I am not too much. I am enough and I am not too much. I am enough and I am not too much. I am enough I am enough and I am not too much. I am enough and I am not too much. I am enough and I am not too much. I am enough and I am not too much. I am enough and I am not too much. I am enough and I am not too much. I am enough and I am not too much. I am enough and I am not too much. I am enough and I am not too much. I am enough and I am not too much. I am enough and I am not too much. I am enough. I am ENOUGH.

The flowers never look for your approval when they bloom,

and nor will I.

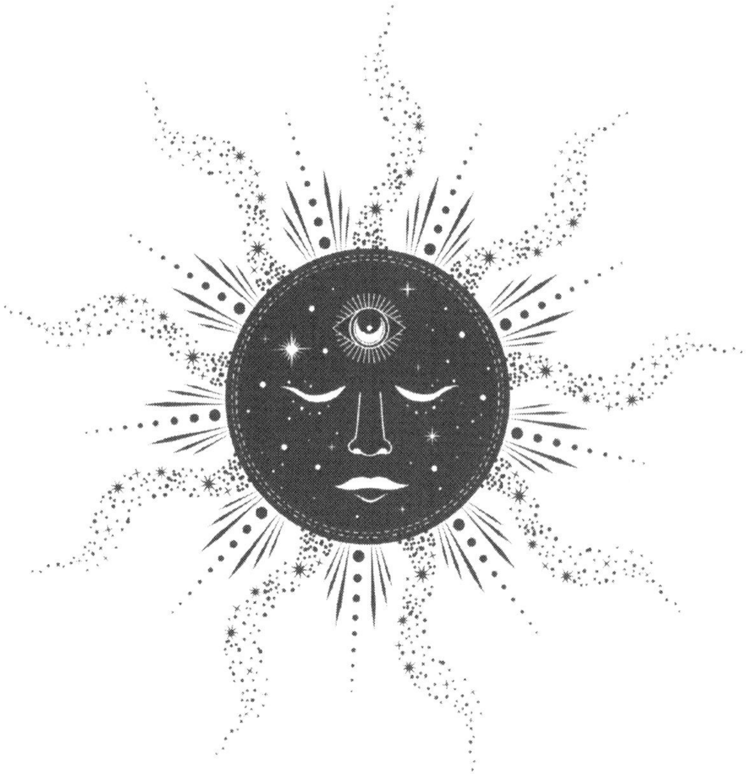

She runs
with wolves and
comes alive in the moonlight.

She needs no man,
for she can save
herself.

SOMETIMES, IT DOESN'T MATTER HOW **BADLY** WE WANT IT. IF IT DOESN'T FIT, THEN IT DOESN'T BELONG.

*Never settle for a love
that
hurts.*

*Even when you're lonely,
even when you cry,
you are always
—always—
beautiful.*

They may have fit you perfectly, but remember, you are soft and flexible and not created for the sole purpose of fitting someone else.

I'm not walking away. I'm walking toward something (someone) better

I WILL NOT ALLOW SOMEONE TO TREAT ME LIKE A *PLAYTHING.* I AM NOT A TOY, I AM A WORK OF ART

Of course it's going to take a while
to feel okay.

Like peeling off a sunburn
to reveal pink skin underneath,

sometimes we must shed a layer
before the new can grow.

Part 2: For self-love

Today I Affirm:

I am strong
and smart
and full of potential

I AM NOT A MERMAID,
I AM THE SIREN-

MY POWER
IS MY VOICE.

(DO NOT FORGET)

You do not get to push me out of the nest, then take credit for teaching me to fly.

You're a little sad
and that's okay

You don't have to be
like the rest of them—

Dark stars shine, too.

I CAN BE
BOTH GRATEFUL AND SAD
IN THE SAME
BREATH—
ONE DOESN'T
CANCEL
OUT THE OTHER.

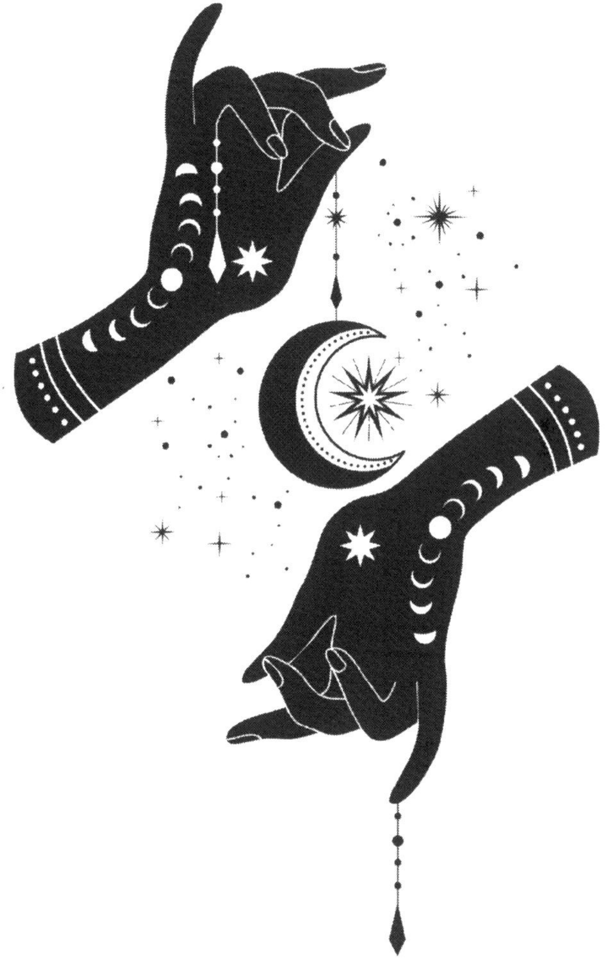

I AM STILL
LEARNING HOW
TO LOVE MY
BODY

AND I'M STILL
LEARNING HOW
TO BE OKAY ON
THE DAYS WHEN
I DO NOT.

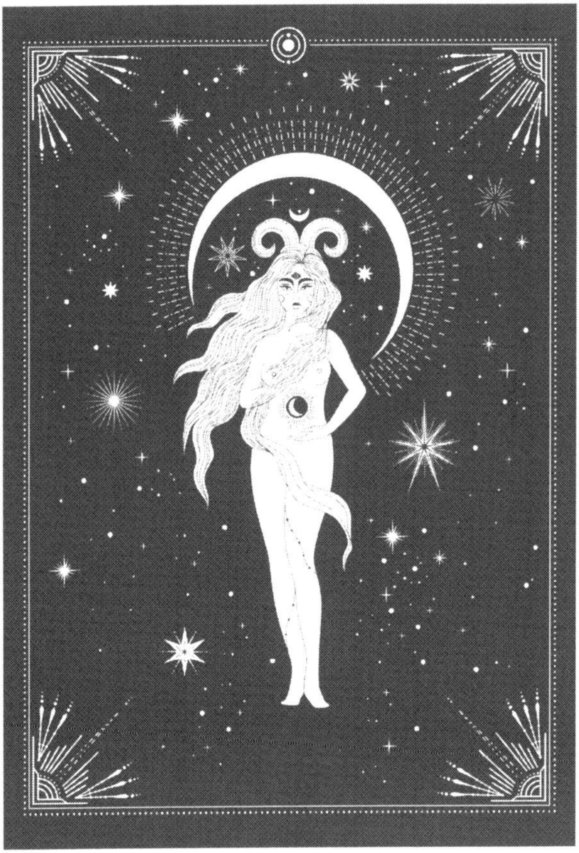

I will not water down my words just because you find my tongue too potent.

Today, I choose to love my body exactly as it is. The stretch marks, the dimples, and all the dips and folds. I choose to love the flat parts, the bumpy parts, the hairy parts, and the drooping parts. I choose to love all of the things society has conditioned me to believe are *imperfections*, but are really the things that make my body *mine.* I choose to love my missing parts and the parts that work differently on me than they do on others. Today, I choose to love my outsides. Though it may not be the most important thing about me, goodness, isn't it beautiful?

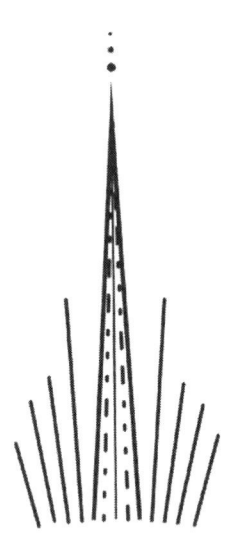

I cannot decide to make today a happy one,
but I can decide to *try*.

She plants her

FEET

and

MOUNTAINS

rise for her.

A CHECKLIST FOR DAILY SELF-LOVE

(IN NO PARTICULAR ORDER)

GET OUT OF BED AND SHOWER	
HYDRATE MY BODY WITH WATER	
CREATE SOMETHING	
GO FOR A WALK IN NATURE	
NOURISH MY BODY WITH FOOD	
TAKE MY MEDS/SUPPLEMENTS	
CONNECT WITH PEOPLE I LOVE	
PUT DOWN MY PHONE-BE PRESENT	
DITCH THE SCALE	
TREAT MYSELF TO A SMALL JOY	
CLEAN MY LIVING SPACE	
DO SOMETHING RELAXING (FACE MASK, PET CUDDLE, READ A BOOK, LISTEN TO MUSIC)	
GET IN BED AT A REASONABLE HOUR	

When the world seems hard, be soft with you.

Accept that someone else can love you even when you cannot seem to love yourself

Like a mountain,
I will rise
in spite of all the men
who think they've
conquered
me.

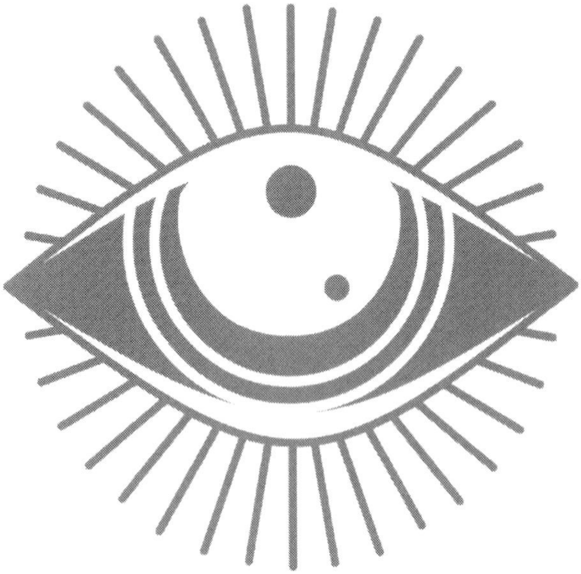

BE PATIENT

WHAT YOU SEEK WILL COME TO YOU.

When you think your tears are for nothing, just remember - when the sky cries, everything grows.

Dear self–

I won't always love you right,
but I will always love you
enough to try.

Sincerely,
still growing

GO AHEAD AND BEND ME IN HALF, LET ME SHOW YOU HOW UNBREAKABLE I AM.

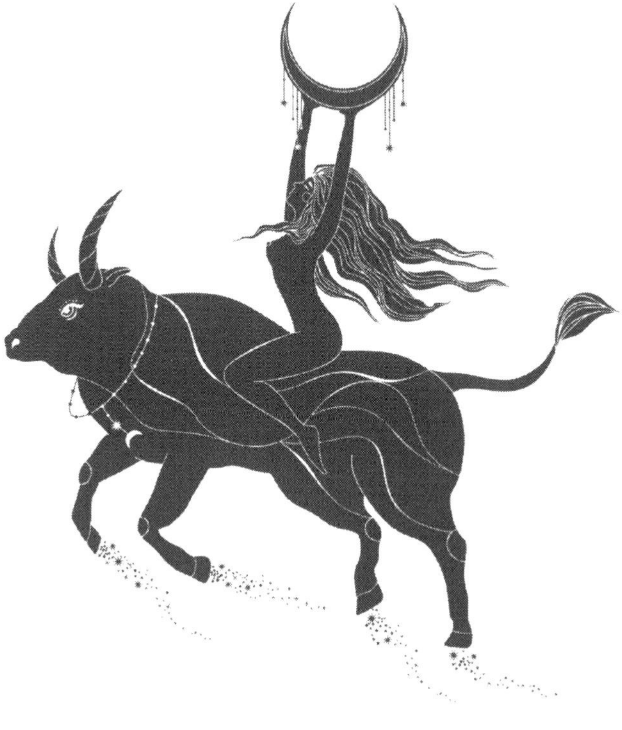

KEEP GOiNG KEEP GOiNG KEEP GOiNG KEEP GOiNG KEEP GOiNG KEEP GOiNG
KEEP GOiNG KEEP GOiNG KEEP GOiNG KEEP GOiNG KEEP GOiNG KEEP GOiNG
KEEP GOiNG KEEP GOiNG KEEP GOiNG KEEP GOiNG KEEP GOiNG KEEP GOiNG
KEEP GOiNG KEEP GOiNG KEEP GOiNG KEEP GOiNG KEEP GOiNG KEEP GOiNG
KEEP GOiNG KEEP GOiNG KEEP GOiNG KEEP GOiNG KEEP GOiNG KEEP GOiNG
KEEP GOiNG KEEP GOiNG KEEP GOiNG KEEP GOiNG KEEP GOiNG KEEP GOiNG
KEEP GOiNG KEEP GOiNG KEEP GOiNG KEEP GOiNG KEEP GOiNG KEEP GOiNG
KEEP GOiNG KEEP GOiNG KEEP GOiNG KEEP GOiNG KEEP GOiNG KEEP GOiNG
KEEP GOiNG KEEP GOiNG KEEP GOiNG KEEP GOiNG KEEP GOiNG KEEP GOiNG
KEEP GOiNG KEEP GOiNG KEEP GOiNG KEEP GOiNG KEEP GOiNG KEEP GOiNG
KEEP GOiNG KEEP GOiNG KEEP GOiNG KEEP GOiNG KEEP GOiNG KEEP GOiNG
KEEP GOiNG KEEP GOiNG KEEP GOiNG KEEP GOiNG KEEP GOiNG KEEP GOiNG
KEEP GOiNG KEEP GOiNG KEEP GOiNG KEEP GOiNG KEEP GOiNG KEEP GOiNG
KEEP GOiNG KEEP GOiNG KEEP GOiNG KEEP GOiNG KEEP GOiNG KEEP GOiNG
KEEP GOiNG KEEP GOiNG KEEP GOiNG KEEP GOiNG KEEP GOiNG KEEP GOiNG
KEEP GOiNG KEEP GOiNG KEEP GOiNG KEEP GOiNG KEEP GOiNG KEEP GOiNG
KEEP GOiNG KEEP GOiNG KEEP GOiNG KEEP GOiNG KEEP GOiNG KEEP GOiNG
KEEP GOiNG KEEP GOiNG KEEP GOiNG KEEP GOiNG KEEP GOiNG KEEP GOiNG
KEEP GOiNG KEEP GOiNG KEEP GOiNG KEEP GOiNG KEEP GOiNG KEEP GOiNG
KEEP GOiNG KEEP GOiNG KEEP GOiNG KEEP GOiNG KEEP GOiNG KEEP GOiNG
KEEP GOiNG KEEP GOiNG KEEP GOiNG KEEP GOiNG KEEP GOiNG KEEP GOiNG
KEEP GOiNG KEEP GOiNG KEEP GOiNG KEEP GOiNG KEEP GOiNG KEEP GOiNG
KEEP GOiNG KEEP GOiNG KEEP GOiNG KEEP GOiNG KEEP GOiNG KEEP GOiNG
KEEP GOiNG KEEP GOiNG KEEP GOiNG KEEP GOiNG KEEP GOiNG KEEP GOiNG
KEEP GOiNG KEEP GOiNG KEEP GOiNG KEEP GOiNG KEEP GOiNG KEEP GOiNG
KEEP GOiNG KEEP GOiNG KEEP GOiNG KEEP GOiNG KEEP GOiNG KEEP GOiNG
KEEP GOiNG KEEP GOiNG KEEP GOiNG KEEP GOiNG KEEP GOiNG KEEP GOiNG
KEEP GOiNG KEEP GOiNG KEEP GOiNG KEEP GOiNG KEEP GOiNG KEEP GOiNG
KEEP GOiNG KEEP GOiNG KEEP GOiNG KEEP GOiNG KEEP GOiNG KEEP GOiNG
KEEP GOiNG KEEP GOiNG KEEP GOiNG KEEP GOiNG KEEP GOiNG KEEP GOiNG
KEEP GOiNG KEEP GOiNG KEEP GOiNG KEEP GOiNG KEEP GOiNG KEEP GOiNG
KEEP GOiNG KEEP GOiNG KEEP GOiNG KEEP GOiNG KEEP GOiNG KEEP GOiNG
KEEP GOiNG KEEP GOiNG KEEP GOiNG KEEP GOiNG KEEP GOiNG KEEP GOiNG

-when anxiety-
BUBBLES

-when the sadness-
ACHES

-we must plant our-
FEET

-furrow our -
BROWS

-and-
MARCH ON.

Alone
is not a dirty word
Alone
is not lonely or waiting
Alone
is just you and sometimes
you
are all you need.

The world has enough sharp edges.
Stay soft, beautiful girl.

LET THIS BE
THE YEAR
I STOP
BELIEVING IN
FAIRY TALES
AND START
BELIEVING
IN MYSELF.

Magic,

Fire,

Stardust,

Grace.

EACH RUNS THROUGH YOUR VEINS,

YOU JUST HAVE TO
FIND THEM.

The anxiety you feel is just a scared little child.
Hold her, dry her tears, and promise
her you've got this.

Because you do.

Grow where you have room to flourish.

Don't force yourself into a garden
that's already been sown.

Repeat after me:

I will never be ashamed of the way
someone else hurt me.

They may have left scars,
but I won't allow them to make
their shame mine.

YOU ARE LUCKY

IF YOU HAVE NO IDEA WHO YOU ARE, FOR YOU CAN STILL BE ANYTHING YOU WANT.

Today,
you owe the world
nothing.

Today,
give yourself
to you.

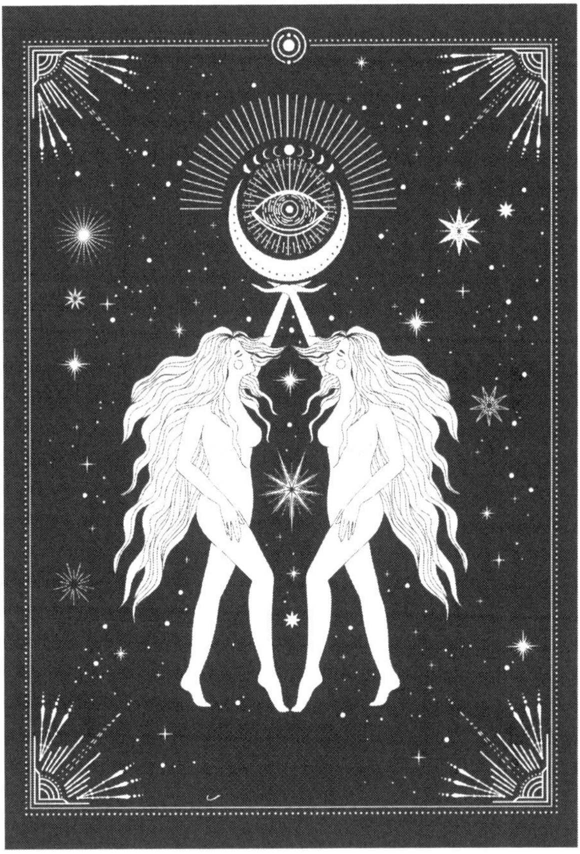

I am not very brave
but I very much try to be
and I think that is enough
for today.

Listen to your soul;
You already know what you need.

IF I CAN BELIEVE ON WISHES MADE ON DUST TRAILS OF BURNING ROCK IN THE NIGHT, I THINK I CAN MUSTER THE COURAGE TO BELIEVE IN

MYSELF.

I ~~SHOULD~~ *WILL*

LOVE MYSELF BETTER

~~TOMORROW~~

STARTING *RIGHT NOW.*

I AM LOVED EVEN WHEN I CANNOT FEEL iT. I AM LOVED.

(REMiNDER)

YOU DESERVE PEACE.

I feel indigo today–
a deep, dark bruise.

I don't feel the ache much anymore,
only the potential to heal.

And there is so much potential.

Today I affirm:

It's okay to visit sadness,
so long as I do not live there.

It's okay to ring the doorbell of heartbreak,
so long as I do not stay forever.

It's okay to lie in bed all day,
so long as I get up tomorrow.

It's okay to take time for myself,
so long as I know I am loved.

It's okay to sink into the anxiety,
so long as I do not drown.

It's okay to break,
so long as I acknowledge that glued-together
shards are just as pretty as they were
before the shatter.

(I WANT YOU TO LOOK iN THE MiRROR AND SEE SOMEONE BEAUTiFUL)

And she proclaimed:

I am the SUN.

YOU ARE SO MUCH STRONGER THAN YOU WERE YESTERDAY; BELIEVE THAT.

Maybe the castles you build keep crumbling down
because you're looking for a prince(ss)
when you should be looking
for yourself.

I DON'T NEED BLOOD
FROM ANYONE
WHO HAS WRONGED ME;
REVENGE IS NOT
A HEALING LANGUAGE.

I MAY

-break-

BUT THEN I'LL

-grow-

Break through those cracks,
you fearless,
radiant little flower.

THE SUN

19

Repeat after me:

It is okay to put myself first...

...and not feel guilty about it.

GIVE YOURSELF PERMISSION TO
OUTGROW RELATIONSHIPS AND
MOVE ONTO THINGS THAT
BETTER SERVE YOU.

(ALL FLOWERS EVENTUALLY
OUTGROW THEIR POT)

You are entitled to the same love you
 so readily give to others.

Perfection is **BORING,** show me your **SCARS.**

Why is it so easy to talk about loving ourselves, yet so hard to actually f!%king do it?

Even the brightest days will
end in twilight,
even the darkest nights
will see the yellow sun rise.

(it gets better)

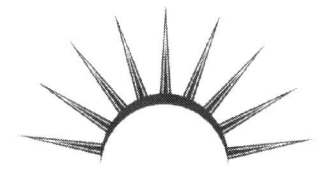

And after all this time-
the endless lonely nights,
rejection that stung like bees,
the sour taste of near defeat.

Here you are rising like the sun herself,
a shining tribute to all the flowers we thought were lost
under the heavy blanket of winter but surprised us by
clawing through on the first of May.

You are the red tulip on Mayday,
and you shall never be uprooted.

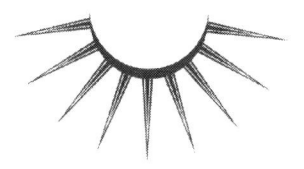

Repeat after me:

I will not give someone else the power to determine how I feel about myself. I will not give someone else the power to determine how I feel about myself. I will not give someone else the power to determine how I feel about myself. I will not give someone else the power to determine how I feel about myself. I will not give someone else the power to determine how I feel about myself. I will not give someone else the power to determine how I feel about myself. I will not give someone else the power to determine how I feel about myself. I will not give someone else the power to determine how I feel.

Get out of bed. Up. Carpe diem. Sieze the day, or at least the moment. Look at the sunrise. Listen to the rain. Feel the beauty in your bones. Draw. Write. Go to therapy. Take your meds, even when you don't feel like it. Breathe in the fresh fall air. There's no easy cure; there probably isn't a cure at all. But you can do one thing for yourself today to take care of you; you can. You can. You. Can.

In case no one has ever told you it's okay to fall apart—

It's okay to fall apart.

I CANNOT IMAGINE THIS WORLD WITHOUT YOU — THAT IS HOW FIERCELY YOU BELONG.

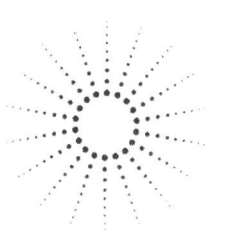

(s)he will never fill you the way
the air can fill your lungs.

Remember-
you are here
for *you.*

I Affirm:

Though I cannot recall the last time I woke up and felt okay, that doesn't mean I won't feel okay again.

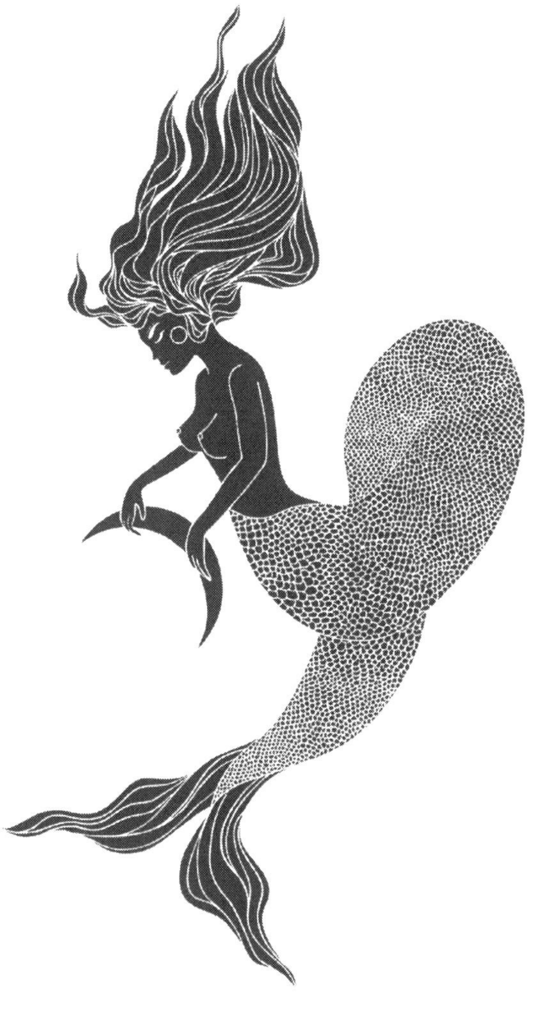

More by Emily Juniper:

FICTION:

Rafa and the Real Boy

POETRY:

A Strangely Wrapped Gift

Things I Learned in the Night

Swim

JOURNALS:

One Day at a Time
(Guided bullet journals for mindfulness and mental wellness)

*Get Sh*t Done*
(Daily planners + organizers)

Find everything by Emily Juniper on Amazon.com

@by.emilyjuniper

Printed in Great Britain
by Amazon